Playing Fast and Loose with Time and Space
by P.S. Mueller

Meadowbrook Press

Distributed by Simon & Schuster
New York, NY

Library of Congress Cataloging-in-Publication Data
Mueller, P.S.
    Playing fast and loose with time and space / P.S. Mueller.
        p. cm.
    1. American wit and humor, Pictorial. I. Title.
    NC1429.M87A4   1989   741.5'973   88-37984
    ISBN: 0-88166-153-8

Simon & Schuster Ordering #: 0-671-67740-3

Production Editor: Sandy McCullough
Art Director: Kelly J. Nugent
Assistant Art Director: Shelagh Geraghty
Production Manager: Pam Scheunemann

Published by Meadowbrook Press, 18318 Minnetonka Boulevard, Deephaven, MN 55391

BOOK TRADE DISTRIBUTION by Simon & Schuster, a division of Simon and Schuster, Inc., 1230 Avenue of the Americas, New York, NY 10020.

89 90 91 92 4 3 2 1

Printed in the United States of America

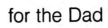

for the Dad

The Truth About P.S. Mueller

I live with P.S. Mueller. I'm a cat. My name is Pooder. It's a good enough life, I guess. He feeds me whenever I hassle him and he keeps the litter clean.

He can be a bother sometimes, though, especially when he's having trouble with a new batch of drawings. He paces around the house for hours, talking to himself and making faces. The other night, I had curled up for a nap on the dining room table and was just drifting off when he descended upon me, babbling and grabbing at my head and saying, "Pooder! You're a cat, you're all covered with fur and you can't help yourself!" When he gets like this I usually just go all rubbery and let him get it out of his system.

But sometimes he's angry about things. That's when he circles the living room, glancing nervously at the television, and telling me that ninety-five percent of everything is crap, that people who desire power over others should be locked up, that Elvis never existed and was created by advertising agencies. I can only take so much of this. After all, my brain is only the size of a walnut.

Most of the time, though, he just sits back in his studio, putting squiggly lines on paper and chuckling quietly to himself. It's not so bad then. I wander the house looking for things to kill or play with, or I sit in the window and look at other cats. He does what he does. I do what I do. It's kind of like a pleasantly dull marriage. Thank God we're both easily amused.

SAFE SEX

WIDOW'S PEAK

THE MAN WHO CAME TO BREAKFAST

ZERO GRAVITY CUISINE
SUNNY SIDE EVERYWHERE

FLAVORING AGENTS

MUELLER

EMPLOYEE—OWNED FRANCHISE

TRENDSETTER

JOHN COUGAR'S MELON CAMP.

JOHN MELON'S COUGAR CAMP

33

SHIRLEY MACLAINE IN HER CAMBRIAN PERIOD

TIME WAITS FOR PEE WEE HERMAN

MUELLER

ATTaché GUEVARA

LOUIE LOUIE AT FORTY

GODOT WAITING FOR
HIS LUGGAGE

HOCKNEY PUCK

MUELLER

GEO-POLITICS 101

NORTH   TRUE NORTH

41

FASHION
STATEMENT

THE FOUNTAIN OF COUTH

LITTLE KARMA SUNSHINE JOHNSON ON HER EIGHTEENTH BIRTHDAY

48

50

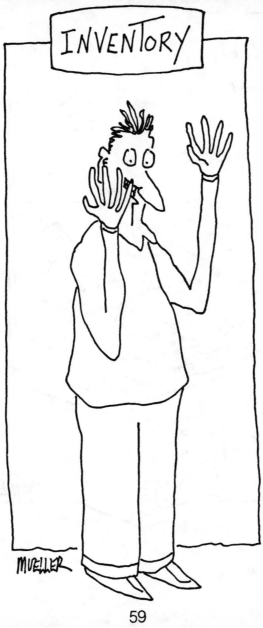

INVENTORY

MUELLER

59

USER
CHUMMY

MUELLER

MARKET CORRECTION

MUELLER

GETTING DIRECTIONS IN LA-LA LAND

CACTICIDE

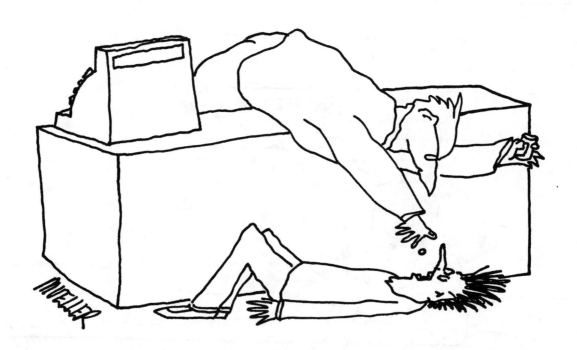

BUSY NIGHT AT THE PIZZA BURN UNIT

MUELLER

72

STRESS TAKES ITS TOLL

MIGRAINES CAN STRIKE ANYWHERE WITHOUT NOTICE

HEIMLICH'S
LAST DITCH
MANEUVER

MUELLER

80

SEDUCED BY TECHNOLOGY

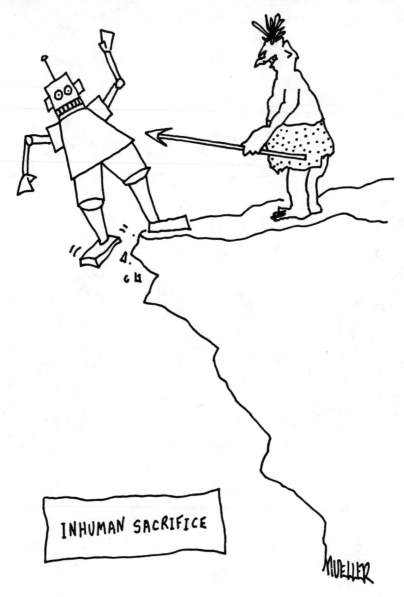

INHUMAN SACRIFICE

MUELLER

PETROLEUM
JELLY

MUELLER

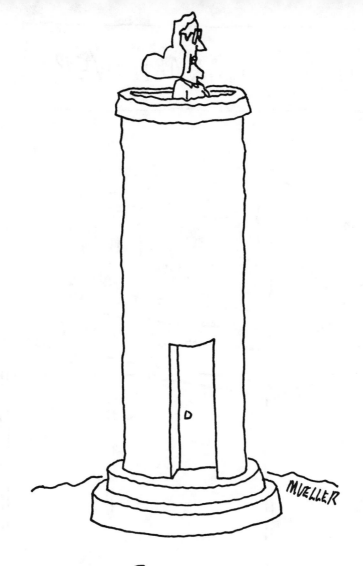

THE TOWER OF MABEL

DEATH WARMED OVER

MUELLER

THE FILING CABINET OF THE GODS

THE DEVIL, HIS ADVOCATE, AND HIS ADVOCATE'S LAWYER

FASHIONABLY LATE FOR THE END OF EVERYTHING

TIME SHARING IN THE WORLD ABOVE

Order Form

Quantity	Title	Author	Order No.	Unit Cost	Total
	David, We're Pregnant!	Johnston, L.	1049	$4.95	
	Don't Call Mommy	McBride, M.	4039	$4.95	
	Do They Ever Grow Up?	Johnston, L.	1089	$4.95	
	Grandma Knows Best	McBride, M.	4009	$4.95	
	Hi Mom! Hi Dad!	Johnston, L.	1139	$4.95	
	How to Find Romance in the Personals	Price/Dana	4020	$4.95	
	How to Survive High School	Lansky/Dorfman	4050	$4.95	
	Italian Without Words	Cangelosi/Carpini	5100	$3.95	
	Letters from a Pregnant Coward	Armor, J.	1289	$6.95	
	L.I.A.R.	Thornton, R.	4070	$4.95	
	Mother Murphy's Law	Lansky, B.	1149	$3.50	
	Mother Murphy's 2nd Law	Lansky, B.	4010	$2.95	
	Papal Bull	Sullivan, D.	4060	$4.95	
	Prof. Pinkerton's Most Perplexing Puzzles	Maslanka, C.	6070	$4.95	
	Wall Street Bull	Lansky, B.	4040	$4.95	
	Webster's Dictionary Game	Webster, W.	6030	$5.95	
				Subtotal	
				Shipping and Handling (see below)	
			MN residents add 6% sales tax		
				Total	

Meadowbrook Press

YES, please send me the books indicated above. Add $1.25 shipping and handling for the first book and $.50 for each additional book. Add $2.00 to total for books shipped to Canada. Overseas postage will be billed. Allow up to 4 weeks for delivery. Send check or money order payable to Meadowbrook Press. No cash or C.O.D.'s please. Quantity discounts available upon request.

Send book(s) to:

Name _____

Address _____

City_____ State_____ Zip _____

☐ Check enclosed for $_____, payable to Meadowbrook Press

☐ Charge to my credit card (for purchases of $10.00 or more only)

☐ Phone Orders call: (800) 338-2232 (for purchases of $10.00 or more only)

Account #_____ ☐ Visa ☐ MasterCard

Signature _____ Expiration date_____

Meadowbrook Press, 18318 Minnetonka Boulevard, Deephaven, MN 55391
(612) 473-5400   Toll free (800) 338-2232